OFFBEAT

Memories of Tynemouth Borough Police and the communities it served North Shields, Tynemouth & Cullercoats

by Ken Banks

FOREWORD

As an ex-member of the County Borough of Tynemouth Police, who travelled far and wide during my service, I always remembered with pride the formative years with the Borough and in particular the many wonderful and interesting characters, both police and civilian who made such a lasting impression throughout my career. It was therefore a pleasure to be asked by Ken to write this foreword to his aptly entitled book.

Reminiscence and nostalgia are the daily diet of everyone of whatever age and generation and this book will certainly generate much of both amongst ex-members of the police service as well as all with an interest in Tynemouth Borough and local history. However it should not just be read and viewed as another book to stir old memories but more as an insight into how the community developed over the decades and how lessons learned can be adapted and used within a modern environment. Within the following pages are many examples which will enhance the readers knowledge not only of how things used to be but, given some thought, how things could be.

Thanks to Ken and everyone who has assisted with his work. We have a valuable and worthwhile addition to the goal of remembering the past to help to resource and enhance the future.

I wish this publication well.

David A. Wakenshaw
PC 50 County Borough of Tynemouth Police, 1967
Ast, Chief Constable – National Crime Squad, 2001

Previous page: County Borough of Tynemouth Police, CID, March 1969.

Front cover: *Top: Police Fire Engine – part of North Shields Carnival in the 1920s.*

Bottom: Equality – Sergeant Ken Banks and newly-promoted Sergeant Pauline Banks, 1974.

Also available from Summerhill Books

Glimpses of Tynemouth, Cullercoats & Whitley Bay

Having a Wonderful Time at Whitley Bay

Glimpses of Old North Shields

North Shields – The Bombing of a Town

Copyright Ken Banks 2010

First published in 2010 by

Summerhill Books
PO Box 1210, Newcastle-upon-Tyne NE99 4AH

Email: summerhillbooks@yahoo.co.uk

www.summerhillbooks.co.uk

in association with the Remembering the Past, Resourcing the Future Project

www.memoriesnorthtyne.org.uk

ISBN: 978-1-906721-31-2

Printed by: CVN Print Ltd, Maxwell Street, South Shields

INTRODUCTION

This is not a history book. Such books tend to present a chronological account of happenings and circumstances in any given field or organisation. As such they are invaluable sources of reference and fact and have been widely and successfully used by researchers and interested persons for many years.

This book is not specifically chronological, it seeks to portray an illustrated and anecdotal account of the former County Borough of Tynemouth Police from its inception on the 1st January 1850 until its demise consequent to amalgamation on 31st March 1969. It seeks to highlight by way of images the part played by the police, not only in law enforcement, but perhaps more importantly, as an integral part of local society over a period of 119 years.

As a means of attempting to achieve

The County Borough of Tynemouth Police Policewomen's Department, March 1969.

that goal, the book is divided into sections, some of which inevitably overlap, each portraying the role of the constable in the community. In that respect it is not a history book but rather a book about history. Having served in the Tynemouth Force from 1954

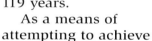

until it became part of the then Northumberland Constabulary in 1969, I began a journey of historical fascination with the police and law enforcement, an adventure which is still ongoing. This book is merely a stopping point on that journey.

Several stations on the journey are highlighted, starting with the early days of the force and progressing through changes in fashion, communication, training, transport, inspection, interaction with the public, investigation, recreation and trivia not always made public, nearing the end of the journey with a tribute to the bravery and courage of force members before finally reaching the end of an era.

Ken Banks
PC 7 Tynemouth Police
D/Sgt 753 Northumbria Police

PC 7 Ken Banks of the Tynemouth Police in 1954.

EARLY DAYS

Mention the words 'early days' to any former policeman and immediately he would think of the 6 am to 2 pm shift. This chapter however is not about shift working, it concerns the formative days of Tynemouth Police, the 'early days' of the force and how it began.

Like many other boroughs and cities, the policing of Tynemouth, or more correctly, North Shields, was until the mid 19th century a haphazard arrangement. The frailties and shortcomings of the early watchmen and parish constables were evident, and as policing in London was becoming structured and organised, the rest of the country looked on with interest to see what could be learned from this new model.

In North Shields in the mid 19th century crime was rife. Murder, muggings, robbery, theft, assault, drunkenness and prostitution were almost the norm on the streets of the 'Low Town' on the riverside. As those who frequented the area were often seamen from all over the globe there was little or no means of controlling their lawless activities. In addition there was a nucleus of residents who also chose to thrive on the proceeds of wrongdoing and the resultant mix proved chaotic, especially for the law abiding townsfolk and business people. The stage was reached where substantial rewards were offered for the return of stolen property and the apprehension of the culprits.

Bearing in mind the London scene and the local criminal chaos, a body of business men in the town met together in 1828 to discuss the issue and also

Sergeant No 1 James Cowan, circa 1870.

other matters of importance to residents – they became known as the Town Commissioners. There was no town hall at that time so a room in the old Gaiety Theatre in King Street was utilised and it was there that numerous important decisions were made. It was decided that a curb on lawlessness may be possible by introducing a number of bye-laws creating petty offences not otherwise catered for by national statute. This became known as the North Shields Improvement Act of 1828 and very useful it proved to be.

By definition, the rules applied only to the bounds of North Shields itself and excluded other areas such as Tynemouth village, Cullercoats, Percy Main, New York and Preston as at the time the County Borough of Tynemouth had not been established. In practice, in later years following the 1849 Charter of Incorporation, the bye-laws were enforced throughout the Borough and indeed remained a useful tool for use by the police up until the 1960s.

The initial problem with the 1828 act was the absence of enforcers, it was beyond the wit or ability of the rare parish constable, and so the Commissioners appointed

A group of Tynemouth Officers – resplendent in their Kepis, circa 1870.

12 men, dressed in long frock coats with reinforced leather collars for protection and similarly reinforced top hats. They were known as North Shields Police. The collars of the men bore the letters NSP and an identification number. Despite radical changes in uniforms over the years the term 'collar number' is used to this day.

The 12 men of North Shields Police seem to have been effective in curbing the excesses of violence and pilfering which had become to many the acceptable norm.

Sergeant (later Chief Constable) Thomas Blackburn circa 1920.

Despite spartan working conditions (they didn't have a police station until 1844) they seem to, by their very presence and demeanour, have had a productive influence in terms of minimising crime and unruly behaviour, the Commissioners' ploy appeared to have worked.

North Shields, as ever revelling in its industrial fortune, soon found that because of development in surrounding areas it was no longer as remote as before. Tynemouth village for example became a continuum of 'Shields' as did the smaller but no less important villages of Preston, Cullercoats, New York, Chirton, Percy Main and East Howdon. As populations grew so too did the qualification the amalgamated areas required to become one single County Borough unit, and on 6th August 1849, the Charter of Incorporation was granted and the new greatly increased area was called the County Borough of Tynemouth but still had a police force of 12 men, plus of course a few diehard Parish Constables who hung on to their meagre authority as long as possible.

The 1st of January 1850 saw the birth of Tynemouth Borough Police, although in reality it was much the same as the former North Shields Force, most of the men transferring automatically. One notable change however was the new 'Chief'. The London model of policing was greatly relied upon and many experienced officers were recruited from the capital to take charge of the new forces which were springing up. Tynemouth was no exception and Robert Mitchell, a senior officer from the Metropolitan force was appointed to take charge holding the rank of Superintendent. As no one else was higher in command, Mitchell was effectively the first Chief Constable, although it was some years before the title of superintendent was changed to that of Chief Constable.

The Watch Committee devised 'Rules and Regulations' for the control of the police and it was the responsibility of the Superintendent, who was required to live in the police station, to ensure they were adhered to. The rules were often harsh, the officers were sworn to carry out their duties to the letter without days off or meal breaks, and to be available, in uniform, for duty at any hour of the day or night. It is understandable that the main breach of the rules involved the taking of refreshment, often of strong drink, while on duty. The penalty for disobeying the rules was usually dismissal.

There is nothing new about expenses scandals much of which has been

A group with Chief Constable Blackburn in 1936.

highlighted nationally in recent times. Back in 1856, when the Tynemouth Force was just 5 years old the Superintendent, who until then had performed a very useful task, was investigated by the Watch Committee following allegations of claiming expenses for men who had attended a fire. None of them received a penny despite the pay sheet having been signed purportedly by them!

As the investigation was drawing to a close the Superintendent left the police station and was never seen again, the Watch Committee were not too pleased and directed that should he ever appear back in the Borough he was to be arrested. He is still at large!

Pending the appointment of a new superintendent, a police constable was given temporary charge of the force, a strange situation when there were sergeants presumably better qualified. In 1857, another Metropolitan man, John Hewitt became the new superintendent remaining in office until his death in 1871. It was during Hewitt's 14 year tenure that a police pension scheme was introduced, and for the first time retiring officers were financially catered for.

Superintendent Hewitt, being conversant with London plans for dealing with frequent rioting, instituted a similar plan in Tynemouth. Rioting in the Borough was infrequent but there were occasions when the plan was successfully put into practice. The Superintendent also created a system of mutual aid between forces should the need arise in addition to a system of 'crime intelligence', a sharing of information on criminal activities between local forces. Interestingly, despite the relatively enormous size of modern police forces, the mutual aid system still operates, even being used at the time of writing.

In 1878, Alexander Anderson became the third superintendent of police at Tynemouth, the force by this time had reached a strength of 48. Anderson had originally joined Tynemouth Police as a constable and rose through the ranks to the highest position, a precedent which was followed in later years by two more men.

Anderson, who was being addressed as 'Chief Constable' by the Watch Committee, instead of superintendent, was an innovative man. During his tenure of office two extra police stations were built, in Lawson Street in the west end and Oxford Street in Tynemouth village as well as a 'lock up' in the Bull Ring, the western extension of what is now the New Quay. He introduced detectives into the force and keenly headed the force ambulance team, men being awarded St John's Ambulance badges worn on the right sleeve.

Mr Anderson championed better conditions for his men and enthusiastically sought to ensure their pay was adequate for their needs. There was no central control of police pay at that time, there was no federation

The Bull Ring, North Shields – the site of a 'Lock Up' for custody of prisoners until transported by cart to Saville Street Police Station.

to look after constables' needs and rates of pay varied from place to place. Anderson, who seems to have had his men's needs very much to heart devised a pay scale which although was meagre, was sufficient to attract the right calibre of recruits. He rewarded proficient service not only financially but also introduced 'service badges', worn on the right sleeve in the form of inverted chevrons so the public could identify constables who 'had some in' to quote recent military parlance.

After 15 years Alexander Anderson died in office, a bitter blow to the force which he had developed and which was flourishing under his command. His successor however was no less diligent and enthusiastic, for John Hall Huish, a Newcastle Police superintendent was equally innovative and responsible for several initiatives which enhanced the performance of the force.

The opening of the Police Club in the muster rooms, 1965.

He seems to have had the welfare of his men very much in mind for one of his first tasks was to change the Police Recreation Association, which although in existence for some years, was seldom used, was devoid of suitable premises, had little or no equipment and no organisation. Within a short space of time rooms above the courtroom had been acquired, renovated, furnished and made functional, the result being the forming of an organising committee, the arranging of social and sporting events in which police families and friends could attend. Very soon the Association was flourishing and personnel became active in its organisation and running. A precedent had been set by Chief Constable Huish, because the Association, albeit in a changed form existed, with the aid of successive Chief Constables' until the last days of the force.

One of the functions of the early police in Tynemouth Borough was to attend fires. This was not an organised response from highly trained fire fighters to attend all fires, there was the all important monetary issue to be considered. Householders and business people tended to guard their premises against fire with insurance policies, much the same as today but with a notable difference!

Those who could afford it paid a premium to insurance companies, and were given a certificate, not a paper document as we are accustomed to, but a metal disc some 9 inches in diameter which the insured attached to the outside of his property where it could be easily seen. Should fire break out in the premises the 'fire brigade', a somewhat grandiose term for a bunch of untrained policeman carrying leather buckets of water and a ladder, would attempt to extinguish the fire, but only if the Insurance Disc was visible. Should there be no disc showing no attempt would be made to put out the fire and the 'brigade' would return to the station!

Watching the birdie rather than the fire in the 1930s.

Tynemouth Police Fire Brigade deal with a car fire in the early 1930s.

STYLES AND FASHIONS

From the outset, police officers needed to be recognised as such. The very nature of their duties demanded that they presented a visible presence to the public going about their everyday lawful business, and could be immediately available to assist or act appropriately when the occasion arose.

In order to achieve that objective, officers were required to wear uniform clothing, designed and manufactured to the specific needs of the force but also distinguishable from other uniformed organisations such as the military. Indeed, when the first policemen appeared on the streets of London following the success of the Bow Street Runners, one of the main causes of objection was the belief that they were no more than an extension of the army and therefore could not be trusted!

Fish Quay 'Pollis', 1880s.

Such spurious thinking was unfounded but probably based upon the fact that many of the first appointed chief officers were ex-military men and the general public feared they would be treated as military minions. Despite the fact that early police uniforms were remarkably similar to that of certain regiments, the fears were never realised, in fact quite the opposite as early 'Beat Bobbies' were drawn from the community in which they lived and mixed well into the populace with very few exceptions.

The early headgear, called kepis, which were of French origin where they are still used by the Gendarmerie, were introduced in Tynemouth by the first superintendent, Robert Mitchell. The hats, of pillbox shape with a leather peak and air vent on the top, bore the coat of arms of the recently formed County Borough of Tynemouth. Originally in cast brass, this badge was used in white metal, chrome and bullion wire forms for the life of the force albeit in a changed pattern over the last few years of existence.

It was not long before the kepi was dispensed with being judged unsuitable for police use as it afforded little protection from either the weather or persons of evil disposition intent on causing harm to the wearer. In addition, the hat resembled that worn by other organisations such as the Post Office and the Quay Masters Staff. In common with many other forces, Tynemouth was influenced by Home Office suggestions regarding the design of headgear.

Military influence played a part in the adopted hat, the Prussian Helmet, still well known today, was introduced. The first public reaction was one of concern, for the new police helmet was almost identical to that worn by many army regiments. However as time progressed the style of the helmet became synonymous with the police of Great Britain and less related to the military.

There have been three basic styles of helmet used by the police over the years – that with a metal rose top, another with a ball top and the third with a 'coxcomb'. Tynemouth Borough Police has used all three!

In the mid to late 19th century Tynemouth policemen were first seen wearing helmets, the design was a close fitting brim surmounted by the traditional dome shape with a black metal rose top ventilator. The hat, which

A 1910 uniform.

PC Milburn – 1935 uniform.

bore the Borough Coat of Arms, now produced in a thick white metal instead of the original brass, was adorned with metal chain fittings, again following military patterns.

As the years progressed subtle changes to uniforms could be seen. A varied pattern of closed necked tunics evolved, some with breast pockets, others with inside pockets where the note book and whistle could be kept. Other styles of tunic had epaulettes others didn't, some had five buttons to the front, others seven. All, however, from 1850 to 1949 bore the officer's number on the collar.

A significant change to police uniforms took place in the late 1940s. Constables and sergeants on day duty were issued with open neck tunics, shirts with separate collars, and black ties. The innovation came to Tynemouth in 1949 when the force wore the outfits for the first time on the occasion of the His Majesties Inspector of Constabulary's visit. Officers of inspector rank and above had worn the tunics for some time but with white shirts. The blue shirts which were a means of differentiating ranks were made of a coarse material and the separate collars were at times uncomfortable, particularly when collar studs snapped. In later years collar attached shirts were introduced making life much more bearable.

The old style high neck tunics were not immediately scrapped, for officers on night duties were required to wear them as were all personnel during winter months. Policewomen wore blue shirts with open necked tunics from the start.

Although at times constrictive, the high neck tunics had their advantages. At training school for example when recruits were obliged to attend breakfast at 7.30 am, it was convenient to get up, put on the tunic over pyjamas, go to the mandatory breakfast and then dress properly afterwards. It was useful in cold weather conditions to be able to take advantage of multiple 'woolies' under the tunic, something which could not be done with the open necked version!

Sergeant Alex Whitehead, who arrested a murderer in Cullercoats, circa 1920.

Two other items of uniform clothing are worthy of mention, the greatcoat and the cape. Greatcoats were substantial. They, as well as the capes were manufactured in a stout Melton cloth which afforded the wearer almost total protection against the elements. On cold winter days they excelled as the button up to the neck style was guaranteed to keep out the cold, and in severe conditions the turn up collar was an added bonus. The downside was their cumbersomeness. If trying to run or engage in exerting activity the coats often got in the way and thwarted an officer's endeavours to carry out his duty effectively. They were very handy in the early hours of sub zero temperature winter mornings, standing still in shop doorways listening for unusual noises.

If they became wet, as frequently happened, the greatcoats took literally hours to dry out. One recalls finishing night duty at 6 am, going home wearing a drenched greatcoat, hanging it up to dry and finding it still damp when going on duty at 10 pm the next night!

The capes were worse! Made of the same Melton material they were designed to keep the rain and snow out which they did effectively. However once wet their weight increased dramatically making them very difficult to wear or carry. Conventionally a policeman would carry his cape, folded up, over his left shoulder when not in use. This too was cumbersome but it afforded some protection from

PC14 Robert Davidson, circa 1936.

the minority who sometimes chose to do battle with the officer! When worn in conjunction with the greatcoat, the cape had the effect of creating a comfortable, cosy and contented constable! The cape had other uses too. It was the custom for the constable patrolling the Fish Quay to be given his 'fry.' This was a perfectly legitimate gesture from the trawler owners to the police, and normally the fish given was quite small, enough for one family meal. At times, the Fish Quay man would give his 'fry' to a colleague who carried it home in the most suitable fashion, under his cape!

Helmets of varying ornamental style had been used by Tynemouth Police for many years until 1939 when the start of the second world war demanded a restraint on easily identifiable uniform features and black was deemed to be more functional. The police helmets were of a cork structure covered with a bland black felt, topped by a black metal rose. The badge was blackened for night use during the war. This style of helmet, known as the 'Home Office Pattern' pertained for many years until May 1963, when the recently appointed Chief Constable, Walter Baharie ordered new style coxcomb helmets

for sergeants and constables, with a newly designed helmet badge. The badge, or plate, was based on the universal 'Brunswick Star' pattern surmounted by the Royal Crown (the first time the Crown had been used in Tynemouth Police insignia, apart from on buttons), with a central circle containing the Borough Coat of Arms and the words 'Tynemouth Borough Police'. For those officers privileged to wear flat caps, motor patrol drivers, station and administration staff, a new cap badge was designed, dispensing with the metal coat of arms, and inspectors and above were also regaled with a newly designed cap badge.

'Who Stole The Fish?' – A CID Officer at Fish Quay, circa 1910.

These changes met with approval by both the police and the public, the general feeling was one of being modernised and being on a level with other local forces whose insignia was similar. Retrospectively it appears that the original cap badge/helmet plate, the white metal Tynemouth Coat of Arms is now sought after as a collectors item, especially the specimens which were locally chrome plated and worn by the contingent of 12 men who attended the Queen's Review of Police in Hyde Park, London in 1953 in celebration of the Coronation.

As the design for the coat of arms was never registered with the College of Arms, it was possible for many organisations to use it. All Corporation Departments incorporated the device into their reports and letter heads and those employees of the Council who wore uniform used a gilded version as a cap badge.

The story is told of a council workman who, after finishing work one evening became somewhat intoxicated and was found slumped in a toilet by a member of the public. The police were called and the man was arrested for his own safety. The irony was that both the Tynemouth Borough Policeman and the council worker wore the same cap badge!

Left: The Borough Coat of Arms. This example is from the former Oxford Street Police Station. It is currently sited at the foot of Front Street, Tynemouth.

"ALL RIGHT SIR"

By the turn of the century Tynemouth Police was well established with over 50 men, and effectively covered the town centre of North Shields as well as the outlying areas of the newly formed County Borough. The great problem was that of communication.

"All right Sir". These words were the traditional greeting of a constable when visited on his beat by an inspector or sergeant, the word 'sir' being replaced by 'sergeant' in the latter case. What did it mean? Sometimes very little, for it was meant to convey to the supervising officer the fact that all was well. The greeting was adapted from the Metropolitan Police's 'all correct', as those who remember the television series *Dixon of Dock Green* will verify.

The truth was that the constable at that precise moment had little or no idea if everything on his beat was 'all right' or not and therefore the words were rather meaningless. Nonetheless, woe betide the officer who failed to address his senior officers in the conventional fashion. The situation was at times farcical for it was not unknown for lifelong friends, one a constable and the other a sergeant to meet on duty and the conventional greeting being passed, after which the conversation reverted to that of friends, first names being used.

What was happening however was a basic means of communication between two officers at a level of mutual respect, sometimes not for the person, but for the rank. The greeting, although meaningless in a functional sense, was preserved throughout the life of the force and became a cherished part of the life of Tynemouth Borough Police.

Police Box, Preston Village in 1930.

One recalls times when total mayhem was taking place, fights galore, broken windows, injuries to participants in the general fracas and gathering crowds intent on making policing difficult. The sergeant would arrive and the first response from the constable was "all right sergeant!"

In the earlier years, the developing force and the rapid merging of the hitherto outlying villages into a single administrative unit, presented problems for the Chief Constable, primarily how to keep in touch with officers patrolling the outskirts and perhaps more importantly, how they could employ the verbal salutation of "all right Sir" and pass on information or seek assistance.

Before the turn of the century when transport was sparse, the effective method of travel, if not on foot, was on horseback. The senior officer of the day would utilise a horse from a local stable and ride to the outskirts of the Borough in order to confer with his men and pass on information, either verbally or in written form concerning current events relating to crime and details of persons wanted or suspected. Likewise the constables were able to acquaint the senior officer of happenings on their beat. When arrests were made and prisoners, some of whom were of a violent disposition, had to be transported to the police station, use was made of a handcart or, depending on the location, a horse drawn cart, also used by Chief Constable Huish in developing the police fire brigade.

The yard at the rear of the Saville Street Police Station was equipped with a robust bicycle stand built to accommodate about a dozen machines. In latter years it was seldom used but when first constructed in the 1890s it served as the base for the force cycle fleet. In those days men still paraded for duty at the police station, regardless of their beat location, where they were updated by the sergeant on the latest

Saville Street Police Station.

information, who was wanted, who was missing, what had been stolen, which dwelling houses were unoccupied and anything else which was considered to be of value to the patrolling constable. Those covering the local beats were marched to a set point while those policing the outskirts would cycle from the station on the substantially constructed Victorian 'sit up and beg' models, the very height of them afforded the rider extra visibility and authority.

The earlier rattles which had been used by officers to attract attention had been discarded and replaced by whistles which could be blown at the discretion of the officer to summon aid or as a warning. The whistle, attached to a metal chain was worn in an inside pocket in early uniforms with the chain showing, and in later years in the left breast pocket, the chain being hooked to the top tunic button. This piece of equipment became synonymous with the police almost to the point of being a badge of office. During the war years however it was similarly used by some branches of the military and local civil defence agencies.

Even after the whistle became defunct with the advent of personal radios, officers still wore their whistle and chain, with I suspect, a deal of pride.

When Mr Huish retired in April 1920, Tynemouth Borough Police had changed dramatically under his command. A new system of beats had been introduced with the advantage of organised administration and command. Two extra police stations, in Lawson Street and in Oxford Street, Tynemouth, had been built which effectively meant that the Tynemouth Force was divided into three divisions, each commanded by an

A 1920s Parade March Past with officers resplendent with World War One medals.

inspector, a new rank which had been introduced, and each with its own cells, charge room and office accommodation. The system lent itself to a level of efficiency hitherto unknown in the force. The missing element as far as communication was concerned was the new fangled system of telephones. This was quickly remedied and a call to 'North Shields 206' from the public telephone system put the caller directly through to the Saville Street police station, which in turn had connection lines to the other two stations. The system was particularly invaluable during the First World War where extra vigilance and methods of contact were necessary.

The early to mid years of the twentieth century were innovative to the extent of changing the lives of everyday folk. Technology was moving forward at a rapid pace and new methods and ideas were prolific, non more than in the field of communication. The prefix 'tele' as an adjective to distance contact was introduced in terms of telephones only at that stage but gradually and then rapidly became the 'in word' of communication. Telegraphs and telegrams evolved effectively and the telephone system became more sophisticated and complex and was the forerunner of such innovations as telex, teleprinters, and television, all of which are now considered as common place and necessary to modern living.

The potential was not lost to police forces. In 1929, the next Chief Constable, Thomas Blackburn, who had joined Tynemouth Police as PC 75 and had risen through the ranks, instituted what was to become a major step forward both in terms of communication and a new level of comfort for the beat officers, the police box.

These wooden structures, each containing a telephone, a desk, a wooden stool and a first aid kit, were placed at strategic points throughout the Borough, usually one box per beat where the beat diary and all documents relating to current police issues were kept. The beat diary included all messages received by telephone from HQs plus any information relating to the beat. Items such as stolen property, vehicles or items of national importance had to be meticulously handwritten, and later cancelled when the property was recovered or the issue resolved.

If a beat constable was required, the telephone operator at HQs was able to flick a switch and an amber, not blue, light flashed intermittently at the beat box. As soon as the constable answered the telephone the light automatically was extinguished, or could be cancelled from the police station if the officer was no longer

Police Box, Foot of Percy Park, Tynemouth in the 1930s.

required. The system was later extended to include a small number of telephone standards situated at strategic points throughout the Borough between police boxes, allowing both officers and the public communication access to police HQs.

In later years, in the 1960s, another innovation was made when the then Chief Constable, James Joseph Scott persuaded the Watch Committee that personnel and efficiency would benefit by the construction of 'section houses', three brick built structures situated at Billy Mill, Linskill Terrace and the foot of Percy Park Road. These buildings still stand today but only the Tynemouth one is in use by Northumbria Police. In addition, about the same time, three large brick built boxes were constructed at Wallsend Road at the junction of Bridge Road North, on Norham Road, near the Coast Road junction and on Hartington Road on the Marden Estate. These boxes had no facilities other than space and the usual telephone. All police boxes had facilities for public emergency telephone and first aid use.

The section houses proved very popular with police officers as they afforded the space for several people to function simultaneously and also act as focal points to accommodate several officers should an incident occur requiring more than the usual number. The houses included washing and toilet facilities and a fully equipped kitchen. The attractive odour of bacon and eggs could often be detected by the passer by or even the less attractive smell of burnt toast, depending on the level of the officer's culinary skills. A gas fire proved a great asset during cold or wet weather, and a level of comfort hitherto unknown to the beat constable was achieved. The section houses accommodated officers from adjacent beats which in practice meant that several could be in the 'box' at any one time and not on their actual beats. However, as bicycles were frequently used and housed in a purpose built part of the section houses, men could very easily be back within their beat boundaries in a short space of time.

The tenure of Thomas Blackburn saw the first use of a motor car by Tynemouth Police. In 1933 an Alvis was purchased by the Watch Committee, the intention being that of a more effective means of travel for the inspector to visit his men. Regrettably within the space of seven months the car was badly damaged in a collision with a tree. The inspector who was driving was not seriously injured but his passenger, a PC, was thrown from the vehicle and killed.

Motorisation was becoming a popular means of transport with the public both as a way of leisure and business travel and police forces were virtually obliged to invest in vehicles primarily as instruments in the enforcement of the ever increasing volume of legislation covering road traffic, and of course an ideal way of enhancing communication between supervisory officers and those on the beat.

The greatest problem with the police box telephone system was that constables and sergeants were required to 'ring in' hourly on a staggered time scale to HQs. This ensured that all was well with the officer but only on an hourly basis. What happened between ringing in times was unsupervised and the constables were

An inspection parade taken in Northumberland Park, circa 1935.

left to their own devices for that period. Of course if anything should happen on his beat the constable could use the box phone for assistance, or a motor vehicle could be sent to deal with the matter, but it was always possible for some harm to befall an officer just after he had rung in and it would not be noticed for one hour. Fortunately such happenings seldom occurred.

The potential problem still existed however, and as technology progressed the use of radios became more prevalent. Tynemouth Police Headquarters, situated in Saville Street was equipped with a Home Office radio, enabling the operator, the station sergeant in the earlier days of the innovation, to contact the then two cars fitted with radio. The system was regulated by Durham Constabulary from Marley Hill, each local force being given a call sign, and each vehicle given an appropriate call sign number. The call sign for Tynemouth was M2LQ, and the cars were M2LQ 2 and 3 respectively, the station having the number 1. In practice the call 'Queenie 1 to Queenie 2' was used soon to become abbreviated to Q 1 to Q2. Whenever the radio was employed either the station operator or the patrol car driver would have to access the system by calling up Northumberland Constabulary headquarters or M2LB and asking for 'talk through'. The system was time consuming and sometimes frustrating should the channels be busy, but it was the best available at the time.

One station sergeant, Fred Millions possessed a particularly loud voice, and when the system was introduced in the late 1940s, he would lift the transmitter and literally shout into the handset – he could be heard a mile away. Maybe the radio wasn't needed for him!

One day in the mid 1960s, the exciting news came that mobile personal radios were being tested by the Home Office for police use. Tynemouth was selected to try out one of the sets. When it arrived it was something of a surprise for it consisted of a bulky 'back pack' with an aerial protruding 2 feet into the air. The monitor was held at the police station and an unfortunate CID officer was selected to try it out. After walking two hundred yards or so he was totally exhausted because of the weight

The 'New look' of 1949 – Tynemouth officers on inspection parade, wearing the open necked tunics and collars and ties for the first time.

of the apparatus. However he duly obeyed the instructions to the letter and called in to Headquarters. Nothing happened.

After repeated attempts to contact the police station, and now totally despondent, the officer decided mobile radios were not the answer to effective communication and the set was returned. No one ever saw that type of radio again!

The idea was not without merit, for after some years of testing, the Pye Radio company came up with a system of personal radios consisting of a two piece set, one transmitter and one receiver which were pocket size and very light in weight. The receiver was clipped onto a tunic and the transmitter fitted snugly into a breast pocket. The radios were battery operated and a battery charging system was fitted in the police station capable of charging some 30 batteries simultaneously. The result was that every officer within the Borough was in immediate radio touch with HQs, a very effective means of communication indeed. The down side was that the batteries frequently needed changing which was tiresome and depending on location, there were times when transmitting proved difficult.

This system of personal radios was still in use when the 1969 amalgamation took place. When first used, a constable took out a radio some distance from the station to try it. The station sergeant called to him, "Control to PC ... How are you receiving me?"

"All right Sarge" was his reply.

The annual inspection in 1964 – 6' 7" PC Roly Craig is talking to the HMI.

'COP CARS AND CARS COPPED'

As the 20th century developed, so too did industry. New techniques and methods began to save time and money as innovations gradually replaced the old. One of the more significant features was the evolution of the internal combustion engine, one only need to look at the congestion of modern day roads to realise the truth of this statement.

The motor car had arrived and with it a fresh approach to everyday living. Early motor transport was crude by modern standards but gradually it began to make its mark in history. Few families were able to afford a motor car in those early days, few families can afford not to have access to one today! Once the so called 'horseless carriage' appeared on Britain's streets it became very obvious that controls over its use were indicated. Horse drawn carts presented little difficulty for the legislators, but motorisation resulted in a plethora of potential problems and the way they were addressed was by ream upon ream of statutory instruments, filling the law books on the lawyers shelves and their pockets as a bonus!

'Ouch' – A Traffic Accident in Walton Avenue, North Shields, in the early 1930s.

Enforcement of the ever increasing catalogue of motoring legislation was difficult. The police of the era were unaccustomed to enforcing laws they knew little about and motoring organisations began to spring up to defend their members against some curious prosecutions. For example the policeman who alleged speeding against a driver merely on observation alone without the benefit of mechanical or technological aid. Various devices were tested but it all came down to the use of a stop watch timing a vehicle over a known distance. Not the ideal weight of evidence perhaps but the best available at the time. Interestingly, in later years when motor patrol vehicles were employed, their speedometers were required to be calibrated, achieved by using a measured mile.

Although many new motor vehicles were taking to the road in the earlier years of the 20th century, the number of police vehicles was not commensurate. In Tynemouth for example there was but a single police motor car. Transport still relied largely on bicycles and it was not until the immediate pre-war years that motor cars were purchased for patrol duties. The immediate effect was a more efficient way of covering the ever increasing housing and industrial development and a means of transporting personnel rapidly to incidents.

The days of the old handcarts for

"How did that happen" – Tynemouth Officers examine an overturned car in the early 1930s.

conveying prisoners were over and motorised vans were employed for this purpose. The police in earlier times were responsible for both fire and ambulance duties, and suitably equipped vehicles, although sparse by modern standards, were taken into use throughout the Borough by police personnel who coped with all emergencies in addition to their normal constabulary tasks.

It wasn't until the post war period that investment was made in new vehicles for Tynemouth Police. The then Chief Constable, Tom Blackburn approached the Watch Committee with a request for funding for the purchase of vehicles to address the ever increasing demands upon the police by the influx of new motor cars and lorries on the Borough's roads. The result was firstly the purchase in 1946 of a Morris Commercial van, FT 5566, adapted for the conveyance of prisoners. With its crash gearbox and uncertain braking system, not to mention the difficult steering mechanism, it served the force well for over 10 years, having carried countless numbers of prisoners, lost dogs, traffic signs and any other task deemed suitable. The van made numerous visits to Durham Prison during that time, conveying persons either on remand or committed to a custodial sentence. The van, although new when

Harry Robinson, a noted mechanic and driving examiner.

purchased, began to show signs of ageing as the mileage increased. Trips to Durham had to accommodate a 10 minute break on the journey home to let the engine cool down, strangely coinciding with the driver and escort's need for refreshment at a roadside café!

When a constable applied for permission to drive police vehicles he had to be tested on FT 5566. Part of the test included driving down Tanners Bank and bringing the van to a halt without using the brakes! Crash gear boxes and double declutching were put to the test as was the potential driver. In 1957, the faithful Morris Commercial was put out to grass ironically as a horsebox, and a new van AFT 570, another Morris, much more up to date, was acquired.

As FT 5566 did nothing to alleviate the increasing traffic problems, two saloon cars were purchased in 1947. Both Austin 16s, they were respectively FT 6110 and FT 6161. These two vehicles were the first in Tynemouth to be equipped with wireless and loud hailers, although no police signs, blue lights or sirens were fitted. The cars performed a useful duty as patrol vehicles until 1952 when they were replaced by the then more modern looking Vauxhall Velox saloons, FT 8510 and FT 8554. The Vauxhalls carried illuminated signs, 'Police' to the front and 'Police Stop' to the rear. The monocoque construction of these cars, although modern in concept was less than practical in use. After only five years in use, weaknesses in body work resulted in leaking in the front seat wells and on one occasion when

The police driving school – Wolsely and Alvis cars in the 1940s.

jacked up for servicing the car buckled at the jacking point and required replacing. That said, it should be noted that many privately owned cars of the same make and age lasted much longer, undoubtedly due to the extra stresses and trauma suffered by the police patrol cars. The Vauxhalls, supported by two utility cars, the Humber Hawk FT 7070 and an Austin A70, FT 7650, were eventually replaced in 1957.

The year 1957 was significant. The Tynemouth Council Motor Registration mark 'FT' was drawing to a close. When the number 9999 was reached the authority, in keeping with national policy, instituted the letter 'A' before the 'FT' from the digits 1 to 999 and then 'B' and so forth. Chief Constable Scott, being aware of the ever expanding police vehicle pool, hit upon the idea of reserving the number '1' for the police fleet. The ensuing years saw Tynemouth Police cars bearing registrations AFT 1 up to KFT 1. Obviously the actual vehicles changed over the period but the '1' registrations were passed on to the replacement vehicles. This pattern being maintained until the 1969 amalgamation, when the newly

The first AFT 1 in 1957 – The Chief Constable's Humber Hawk.

formed Northumberland Constabulary, comprising Northumberland County Constabulary, Newcastle City Police and Tynemouth Borough Police, took over all the vehicles. The unique registrations were sold as collectors items as and when the cars were scrapped and can still be seen today all over the country on a wide range of private vehicles.

The first AFT 1 was a gleaming black Humber Hawk, used exclusively by the Chief Constable, although Mr Scott was not keen on driving himself. One evening, in the charge room he said to one young constable, who remains anonymous but whose name features prominently in this book, "Can you drive AFT 1?" "Yes, Sir," was the eager response. "Have you driven it before?" he said. "No, Sir," was the reply. "Then how do you know you can drive it?" said the Chief. The fact that the constable had experience of driving many vehicles seemed to bear fruit as Mr Scott said "You'd better drive me home then."

The experience of driving the Chief's brand new Humber was exhilarating and the temptation to return the car to the garage by the scenic sea front route was great, but as every mile of every police vehicle had to be accounted for, common sense prevailed!

An interesting and amusing aside arose from the No 1 system. A local business man was extremely keen to acquire the number HFT 1. The Chief Constable would not concede and the business man was contented with HFT 2, the number HFT 1 being allocated to a Le Velocette motor cycle and eventually a Bedford 'Panda' van. One of the CID cars, a Ford Anglia Estate, was finished in light blue, minimising its identity as a police vehicle, unfortunately the game was given away

The first BFT 1 – A brand new Austin Westminster in 1959.

18

when it bore the registration plate AFT 1!. Altogether 17 vehicles bore the number '1' plates from 1957 until 1969.

During the war years legislation permitted privately owned motor cars to be requisitioned for military purposes, in some cases this extended to the police who also had control of the ARP (Air Raid Precautions), and suitably camouflaged cars were virtually conscripted into use. As hostilities ceased so too did the legislation and vehicles were returned to their owners. There were occasions however when police officers, patrolling on foot needed to relocate quickly to attend emergency incidents. Walking was not an option due to the distances sometimes involved and cycles were not always available. Officers had statutory power to stop any vehicle but could not lawfully commandeer a car

An inspection of vehicle fleet and drivers in 1964.

as a rapid way of responding to the occurrence. They did, however, ask the driver for a lift. On the very few occasions this was needed, few drivers refused, although they could, by law, have declined the constable's request.

Since the introduction of the breath test and quantitative analysis of driver's blood, incidents of driving whilst 'over the limit' have dramatically dropped. Before the days of the 'breathalyser' if a police officer suspected a vehicle driver of being under the influence, he had power to stop the vehicle and assess the driver's condition. If the driver appeared to be incapable of having proper control then the policeman had the power to arrest him and take him to the police station where he was examined by the police doctor, who subjected the prisoner to a series of tests after which he formed an opinion of his condition and made a statement to that effect, being called upon to give evidence before the magistrates at a later date. Many drivers were described in court as being 'borderline cases' and were dealt with by the bench accordingly. The system was flawed as it relied solely on opinion without the support of analytical testing.

CID Car AFT 1 in 1965. Despite its light blue colour, the registration plate revealed the identity of the Ford Anglia.

Should a driver be arrested on suspicion of drunk driving, his car had to be taken care of and was driven to the police garage in Tyne Street and locked away until the owner was fit enough to drive. The situation was probably the only time a policeman had the opportunity to drive a Rolls Royce!

One of the major problems with immediate post war cars was their limited battery charge, especially when only used for short spasmodic journeys as police vehicles were. Often one of the utility cars would stand for hours outside the police station, only to be used when absolutely necessary. When that occasion arose it was frequently found that the battery was flat and the car wouldn't start. Fortunately, nearby Norfolk Street was on an incline and a push, often assisted by passers by, would be sufficient to start the car! Modern cars have automatic chokes which work effectively, but the 1950 Humber Hawk FT 7070 was not so compliant. It was one of the first to be equipped with such a system, which in its infancy proved to be hazardous, making starting difficult.

In the 1950s and '60s there were still many pre-war vehicles on the road in private ownership. It was becoming difficult and sometimes expensive to maintain them so it was not unusual to see them dumped on waste ground throughout the Borough. They were a cause of annoyance to the police as time consuming enquiries had to be made to trace owners and as they often presented a danger to the public, especially adventurous children. Steps had to be taken to remove them to a safe place, usually the local scrap yard.

Those cars of the era which were still used presented a different sort of problem. They had, in many cases, lacked suitable servicing and maintenance and became un-roadworthy. There were no MOT tests then so the police needed to be vigilant in order to prevent potential disasters. Some officers were specially trained as vehicle examiners and were called upon to examine potentially un-roadworthy vehicles, suspect vehicles maybe used for criminal purposes, stolen vehicles and others which were suspected of having being given unlawful new identities. There were various ways of carrying out examinations, but one basic method of effectively searching the underside of vehicles was contrived by Don Wardhaugh, the innovative and inventive detective who devised a gadget based on mirrors and lamps enabling the under-parts of vehicles to be seen without as much as bending down!

At one stage the CID used an Austin A70, FT 7650 equipped with radio and little else. Don produced a small black box which unobtrusively rested on the rear shelf of the car, but which was

'All the 1s' – A line up of The Tynemouth Police Vehicles bearing the Reg No 1 in 1969.

connected to the electrics and when a button was pressed it showed the illuminated sign 'POLICE STOP'. Several drivers of suspected vehicles were apprehended as a consequence even though the occupants of the police car were all in civilian clothes, querying the legal obligation of suspect cars drivers to stop. No one complained!

When the re-organisation of policing took place in the late 1960s and amalgamation was the national theme, Tynemouth Police lost not only its identity but also its vehicle fleet. In the years immediately prior to the 1969 amalgamation the 'unit beat system' had been adopted which necessitated the purchase of a small fleet of 'Panda Cars'. They were actually Bedford vans and served well despite the heavy usage and frequently snapping clutch cables!

'THE PEOPLE'S POLICE'

One of the great benefits of being a member of a small borough force such as Tynemouth was knowing the people who resided or traded in the area. This asset was further enhanced by the beat system employed. The Borough was divided into small units or beats, few at the beginning but rising to 22 when the 1969 amalgamation took place. The beats were manned for either 24 hours per day or 16 hours depending on location and the number of business premises located on the beat, for example a warm sunny bank holiday (they did happen, but rarely) would attract hordes of visitors to the sea front at Tynemouth between the bathing pool and Cullercoats. The presence of at least two police officers was needed, whereas when darkness fell there were very few people about and the only property to be supervised was the Plaza, the Bathing Pool and the Park Café. This did not warrant 24 hour coverage and the area was well served by officers from adjoining beats.

By far the greatest weapon in the armoury of the beat constable was his interaction with the folk on his patch. The astute officer would very quickly get to know who lived where, what they did for a living, who traded what and where, and of course the everyday problems they faced. At first it may seem that the local 'copper' was prying into affairs which did not concern him, and maybe that was sometimes the case. In fact quite the opposite was true as once accepted into the community, the 'bobby' became a focal point of advice and guidance on matters far outside the content of the training school textbook.

He, and sometimes, she, was the first point of contact simply because they were there, could be seen frequently on the beat and were regarded by some of the residents and business folk as the fount of all knowledge – 'he's bound to know' was the attitude and in most cases that was correct. As far as the police officer was concerned this relationship with the public formed part of a significant learning

The Fish Quay Carnival in the 1920s – the policeman is in control.

curve. When a newly appointed policeman, in his early 20s was let loose on the streets with a limited amount of knowledge of people and even less experience of them, it was not long before important lessons were learned about human behaviour and how to deal with it. In some neighbourly conflicts the policeman was the one to resolve it without 'fear or favour' as he was sworn to do. He had to make instant decisions without being partisan and aim to appease all the participants. In practice it was quite remarkable how this was achieved, maybe the sight of the uniform, worn in those days with the impressive helmet, or the legal powers the officer possessed was sufficient, whatever, the objective was achieved in most cases.

If a beat constable could not readily be found, and such times were rare, a member of the public wishing to see him had only to put a note through the police box door and the matter would be attended to promptly over a cup of tea. In fact the cup of tea was the catalyst in many a delicate situation.

Tynemouth Police Officers were objectively encouraged to participate in the activities of the community. It was sometimes frustrating for a supervisory officer to discover a PC sitting chatting over a cup of tea rather than patrolling his beat, but when it was recalled that the supervisors had done exactly the same thing themselves in their days as constables, and had learned from it, then nothing further was said.

The local policeman was seen by most of the community he served as belonging to them, only those whose activities were suspect tended to avoid the 'copper'. There were of course some people who chose to engage in activities outside the law who befriended the policeman. I recall some whose nature it was to commit crime, but aside from their recidivistic tendencies were no different from others and actually welcomed the policeman in their homes for a 'cuppa'. There were times when it was humorous rather than uncomfortable when visiting a house to see and hear certain goods and commodities being hidden away, out of sight of the copper!

Escorting the 1948 Sunday School Union Good Friday Parade.

Integration with the public is vital in effective policing and in the Tynemouth Borough days this was achieved in several ways. One of less pleasant tasks the beat officer had to perform was delivering bad news, especially involving sudden death. How can anyone sympathetically yet satisfactorily tell the family of a person who has been killed about their unexpected bereavement? There is no immediate answer, it is not in the text books, it can't be taught. It is the product of experience, experience that begins when every constable delivers his first death message. There is no means of knowing how the bereaved will take the news. Seeking support of a neighbour was an acknowledged way of helping the situation, but it was down to the officer to actually break the news.

Probably the worst scenario in this respect was one Christmas Eve when a vehicle overturned and one of the occupants, a young man, was thrown out and fatally injured. His widowed mother was told of the tragedy and took it stoically but one wonders what happened when the front door closed. It certainly marred any festivities the lad's family or indeed the officer, had planned. It was the custom when Tynemouth Infirmary and Preston Hospital were in operation, for the ward sister to seek the help of the police when a patient was so seriously ill that family had to be informed. It was often the case that when such a 'hospital message' had to be delivered the patient was extremely ill and much tact was required in informing relatives, but then policemen were expected to be tactful. It was never the most pleasant of duties to perform, and when the orange light flashed on top of the police box, one hoped that whatever the reason it was not a hospital message to deliver.

PC Jack Short was a practical officer, as a former wartime RAF pilot he was prepared for any contingency, an asset to any policeman. His talents were called upon one night as he patrolled in Bridge Road North. A resident, an elderly man, rather agitatedly called to him. Jack went to investigate and the man said "the lights have gone out". A quick examination by Jack revealed what he expected, a blown fuse. A search of his pockets produced a card of fuse wire and the house was once more quickly illuminated. The grateful resident, quite rightly, thought policemen were wonderful and copious supplies of tea and coffee became available thereafter to any passing officer. The early watchmen and constables trimmed street lamps whilst on their rounds, Jack did much the same thing!

The public often enlisted the aid of the police in many areas. For example a Crime Prevention Department was established which resulted in its two officers

Road Safety Instruction in the infants school 1949 – Inspector Newsome and Sergeant Robinson.

visiting both business and private premises giving advice on all aspects of protecting property. This form of integration with the public proved very popular and many bonds were forged with the police as a consequence.

Talks were given to schools on a wide variety of relevant topics by police officers. There was no method of measuring the success of the exercise but it is likely that even today former pupils will remember the policeman and often a policewoman visiting the school – if nothing else it was better than maths! PC Robert Reay, from the Traffic Department could often be seen in school yards instructing scholars in the art of cycling. Obstacles resembling road hazards were erected and pupils were taught the correct procedures in overcoming them safely. In fact a Cycling Proficiency Certificate was awarded to those pupils meeting the high standard he set. I wonder how many of them in later life, when taking their driving test, remembered what they had been taught, for at that time, Robert, now retired from the force, was a driving test examiner!

Tynemouth Borough Council took pride in its community activities. Summer time swimming galas with the 'Miss Tynemouth' competition; sporting events, in particular the November road race, carnivals which gave the younger population the opportunity to dress up, and the older ones the excuse, if one were needed, to let their metaphorical 'hair down'; post war open air dancing and entertainments; and, in the 1950s the year's highlight – the flower show on Beaconsfield.

All of these activities were supervised by the police who were detailed to attend to ensure the safety and security of those participating. The flower show which ran over three days in early August attracted visitors and exhibitors from all over the North of England, but no exhibitor was more eager to succeed than those from Tynemouth Police whose gardening skills were evidenced at the show. Indeed there is one photograph (see page 40) that shows the police van with three constables at the show. It was not there to transport miscreants from the show to the police station, but rather to transport exhibits from the station to the show!

Inspector Wilf Newsome and Sergeant Harry Robinson instruct pupils at Ralph Gardener School in the craft of road safety, 1949. The tallest pupil in the picture, Gordon Southern, later joined Tynemouth Police.

The annual Good Friday Procession of Witness organised by the Sunday School Union marched through the towns' streets and was supervised by constables at every junction to ensure the free passage of the parade.

Similarly, whenever elections were held, both local and general, officers were detailed to man polling stations. There were insufficient on-duty personnel available to carry out the task so it gave the opportunity for men on leave to perform overtime duty to earn extra money. It was a long day, starting at 6 am and not finishing until the last ballot box had been delivered to the count, which was sometimes near to midnight. In order to ensure full police presence at all polling stations, rest days were cancelled and officers needed to supply themselves with sufficient sustenance for the whole day, there were no breaks.

This then was the involvement of Tynemouth Police in the community it served. Even in wartime the force included itself among the many other organisations who contributed to the 'Wings for Victory' and the 'Salute the Soldier' funds, gaining certificates of recognition which hung on the Chief Constable's wall for many years.

Tynemouth Police officers were the peoples' police officers in many ways. They individually needed to be counsellors, philosophers, psychologists, advisors, peacemakers and sometimes prosecutors. Tasks they performed over the years with sensitivity, firmness and even courage, but above all, common sense.

'WHO DUNNIT'

One of the main tasks of the police is a mission of discovery, who did what? Why did they do it? What was the motivation for doing it and who encouraged it in the first place? The list is endless but whenever a police enquiry is launched such questions are inevitable and seemingly inexhaustible. As with every question, an answer is required and that answer is often easier attained by the employment of specialists. Historically the police addressed the problem by appointing officers specifically to detect criminal activities and organise what today is called a database of information, but in earlier days was known as the Criminal Record Office, every person convicted of crime being given a lifetime CRO number and fingerprint file.

The appointed officers, firstly in London and then in the provinces were called detectives and belonged to a branch named the Criminal Investigation Department. The CID, as it soon became known were not well received at first. Policemen in civilian clothes? – how un-British! Regarded as nothing more than snoopers, the first detective officers did not have an easy life, however as time progressed and crimes were seen to fall in number, their presence was eventually accepted, albeit with some suspicion. The most effective way of crime detection is to meet recidivists on their own territory, a difficult task for an officer in uniform! Having become an established part of London policing in the latter part of the 19th century, CID officers were appointed in the cities, boroughs and counties soon afterwards, indeed photographic evidence shows Tynemouth CID men, resplendent in their bowler hats in the 1880s. Other images taken over the years since then show the presence of CID or 'plain clothes' men among their uniformed colleagues. The term 'plain clothes' is somewhat deceptive as detective officers often appeared in the most garish garb. Indeed in order to mix with criminal gangs, a group of London CID men once dressed up

Helmets, Kepis and Bowlerhats in the 1870s.

as street traders and road diggers, which proved to be an effective ploy!

Tynemouth CID, although primarily formed to detect crime, expanded over the years to include Crime Prevention Officers, Coroners and Warrant Officer, Scientific Aids Officer, which included photography and fingerprints, Aliens Officer, Port Immigration Control Officer, working closely with Customs and Excise, Courts Officers and High Court Liaison Officer. No matter what their role, each had an investigative part to play in the overall efficient running of the CID. From a meagre two detectives at the start, the branch developed a staff of 29 at the point of amalgamation.

Each time a crime was reported to the police, entry was made into the 'Crime Complaint Book' and an initial investigation was made by the recording officer. CID officers were on duty from 8.30 am until 2 am the following morning in staggered shifts, so were usually readily available to assist with the immediate enquiry. On commencing duty in the morning the detectives would examine the crime complaint book to prioritise the order of enquiry. When a member of the public reported a crime by telephone, an officer, often the beat PC, attended initially. Depending on the severity of the reported offence CID officers would visit the scene together with the Scientific Aids Officer as a matter of urgency and in order to minimise disruption of the crime scene. There were instances when serious crime was committed, for detective officers to work round the clock and sometimes all of the following day in order to arrest the culprits. They still couldn't go off duty as case preparation had to be made to place before the magistrates.

When crimes were recorded and details taken, the MO or 'modus operandi' of the offender were important to note. Often correctly interpreted as 'method of operation', the ways and means by which crimes were committed often formed a pattern leading to the identification of the culprit. Then the real work started, first of all finding him and piecing together all the available evidence in order to secure a successful prosecution. Some offenders were cooperative and admitted their guilt straight away, others were more reticent, saying, as was their lawful entitlement, absolutely nothing!

Crime investigation was demanding, time consuming and tiring. One novel method employed to recharge batteries in the middle of an enquiry was to gather in the CID office, stop work, move all the desks to the side of the room giving a reasonable space in the centre, roll up a paper ball and play football for 10 minutes. No-one won the game but everyone was relaxed, tensions released and ready to start work again!

Murder was an infrequent occurrence in Tynemouth, although it did happen from time to time, the usual pattern was that it had its roots in some domestic issue or other. However there were occasions when this horrendous crime was committed without any evidence of familial history or prior knowledge of the victim by the perpetrator. One such case in the 1960s comes to mind when a young lady was found murdered. Initial enquiries ruled out any domestic or occupational involvement and, in order to expedite the enquiry, the Chief Constable asked for the assistance of the Metropolitan Police Murder Squad.

'Calling in the Yard' was a fairly common ploy adopted by many provincial forces at the time as local resources were limited. The 'Yard' detectives were no more efficient than our own, but they had the advantage of an enquiry system. This was the product of many years of murder investigation, based on a card index method which, when operated, collated all the information gleaned from routine enquiry and produced several names of potential suspects. In the case of the Tynemouth murder, the offender was highlighted by the system on almost a dozen occasions. He was arrested, tried and sentenced.

The Scotland Yard team comprised a Detective Superintendent and a Detective Sergeant who, with their experience led the investigation from a purely objective viewpoint. They had the advantage of moving around the country from force to force and were able to use the knowledge gained in any subsequent enquiry. They worked closely with the local officers

PCs Alan Hudspith and Bob Thompson, with Lariat.

holding frequent 'case conferences' in the old Norfolk Street Fire Station which had recently been acquired by the police as an annexe to the Saville Street building. The Scotland Yard men were good mixers and many Tynemouth officers gained useful experiences from their visit.

Discovering 'who dunnit' whilst mainly the province of the CID was not exclusive to them. In keeping with other local forces Tynemouth recruited its first police dog, an asset to initial investigation when a suspect was still in the area of a crime. Lariat, the first dog, handled by Alan Hudspith, was adept at sniffing out people hiding, being trained to bark on discovery. He was joined by Herra, handled by Joe Gunn and a succession of others handled by Maurice Potter and Brian Reed. Many crimes were detected and stolen property recovered by the dogs, crimes which may have remained unsolved or taken many hours to investigate. Indeed, Joe Gunn, and Herra, a massive German Shepherd, were called out to a disturbance in William Street one night where a man was armed with a gun. The man was wanted for several crimes, and when confronted with the police dog attempted to fire his gun but was not quick enough. Herra was well trained and well handled and knew exactly what to do. He grabbed the man before any harm could be caused, his only error was in a misjudgement of anatomical location, he should have bitten him on the arm!

An amusing incident took place in the early hours of one morning at Tynemouth Golf Club where an intruder alarm had recently been installed. Alarm systems had a tendency to activate for no obvious reason and police had to respond to each one rapidly, just in case. On this occasion two officers attended an alarm call and on examination, they found a window broken and a man prowling inside. The clubhouse is far too large to be surrounded by two policemen, so being enterprising they devised a plan. Firstly, backup was called including the on duty dog handler, but as the intruder showed signs of escaping when the alarm bell sounded, one of the constables, with a deep voice, mimicked a dog barking. The intruder was petrified, giving himself up and expressing his dislike of dogs especially if he was about to be bitten! The real dog arrived at the scene and the man was arrested, thinking the dog had been there all the time!

Assistance from the River Tyne Police was always available.

The waterfront at North Shields has a magnetic attraction for many people – those relaxing on a warm day, young boys fishing with a piece of string and little else, fishermen mending nets, the one time early morning throngs on the fish market, buying for their customers, others stealing for themselves and of course the River Tyne Police. The RTP was a none Home Office force, administered and funded by the Tyne Improvement Commission. Their officers were fully sworn constables and had full police powers which were more than useful at times when crime occurred on the river side. The Borough Police were responsible for investigating such offences but it was of little use if the culprit was sailing up river in some makeshift boat to unload stolen property elsewhere. The RTP were called upon to assist on these occasions and were often able to arrest river bound offenders. Although the HQs of the RTP was at Mill Dam, South Shields, they frequently used the Fish Quay or the ferry landing at North Shields to land, and as both of these locations were in the Tynemouth Police area. Rapport with the 'River Lads'

On board the launch with North Shields in the background.

was excellent. The assistance was reciprocal as often late night ferries carried intoxicated passengers who were dealt with by the 'Borough Men' in the absence of a RTP officer.

One of the more delicate areas of investigation concerned females and young children and no one was better equipped to deal with enquiries where detail coupled with sensitivity was called for than the policewomen. There were times of course when female prisoners could be as violent, if not worse than the male. Ask the constable who had a hatpin stuck in his eye by a drunken woman! In such cases male officers were usually required to carry out the arrest and the placing of the suspect in the cells, but always accompanied by a PW.

PWs Pauline Blair and Clarrie Dunn talk to a swimming celebrity at Tynemouth Pool gala.

Policewomen were first employed in Britain in the first world war period when literally thousands of young girls worked in the munitions factories which sprang up around the country, principally in Birmingham, but later, strangely in Gretna. Women officers were appointed but without the powers of male constables, and patrolled in pairs followed some 20 yards behind by a male officer! Some impact must have been made for despite objections from certain chief constables, more and more women were recruited, In Tynemouth there were no PWs until 1945, and even then, Mary Bulman, fresh from war service in the ATS, was appointed, not as a police officer but as a member of the Women's Auxiliary Police Corps, in other words she had a uniform but limited powers. One year later however, the WAPC was abandoned and Mary was sworn in as Tynemouth Policewoman number 1. The PW's formed a separate branch of the force unlike today when women are appointed as constables the same as their male colleagues.

Since the 1946 recruitment of Mary Bulman, Tynemouth Police appointed a total of 13 women including the first sergeant, Mabel Ashley. Following the amalgamation in 1969, the policewoman's department was disbanded and all of the former Tynemouth PWs competed for promotion, with success, throughout the force area on level terms with the men. A far cry from the first decade of women officers who although performing staggered shifts of seven and a half hours compared to the men's eight, often all night, were paid only 90% of the male officer's wage.

The combined talents of the uniform branch, dog handlers, policewomen and the River Police ensured the CID were fully supported in the never ending quest for 'who dunnit'!

'CONSTABULARY CAPERS'

Police Officers, particularly in the days when they were obliged to wear helmets with their imposing uniforms, exuded an air of authority and powerful control. They were stern beings obviously not given to humour or joviality of any kind. How wrong! The fact is that police officers, like anyone else, are appreciative of the funnier side of life as well as being inventive.

Humour and good will were essential qualities if a constable was to carry out his duties efficiently, without fear or favour and maintain the support of the populace. How else would a policeman called to a domestic disturbance where cups and plates were flying across the room and the vocabulary was non dictionary, deal with it? He sat down in the middle told the warring man and woman to be quiet, put the kettle on and make a cup of tea. When this was achieved and peace was restored he suggested, indeed insisted, that they both go upstairs to bed. They both strongly resisted this command, very wise for they were actually next door neighbours! How was the officer to know?

It was common practice in the days of the double decked buses with a rear access platform for policemen to ride on the step from stop to stop. One day PC Gordon Russell, who lived on the Marden Estate was due on duty in the town centre at 2 pm and decided to go by bus. When the vehicle arrived he stood on the back step and all was fine until Preston North Road was reached, the 'bus came to a standstill and moved no further. As time was important the constable alighted from the 'bus to investigate. At the front of the vehicle he found a large horse, refusing to budge. He tried his limited knowledge of equestrianism by cajoling, shoving and shouting, but nothing would make the animal move. Exasperated and being aware of time, he boarded the bus and asked if anyone could help. A diminutive young girl stepped forward, she approached the horse and whispered to it. It moved immediately, back to a nearby field. A rather embarrassed constable thanked her and went on duty!

An early Police Fire Brigade with horse drawn cart.

The same constable had no cause to be embarrassed one night in the town centre where, whilst on patrol, he heard an unusual noise coming from the direction of Lower Bedford Street. He quietly made his way to the area where he saw two men lurking in the shadows of a shop doorway. Despite his furtive approach the men saw him and ran off. A chase ensued through the lanes and streets of the area until eventually the officer caught up with the men near Borough Road. They were almost exhausted, the constable was not! He marched them to the police station, the men still breathless, when inside one of the men asked the station sergeant "Who's he?" pointing to the PC. "Oh," said the sergeant, "he's the best athlete on the force"! It turned out later that the shop had in fact been broken into.

"Keep an eye on the fish", the sergeant said to the constable new to night shift on the fish quay. This command was unnecessary as everyone knew that fish had a habit of disappearing during the night. However, true to his duty, the PC whilst observing the catch being landed lost a contact lens. It was never found but no one could say the constable was not obeying instructions to the letter!

One day whilst taking refreshments in the section house at the foot of Percy Park Road, two constables received a call for assistance at a nearby incident. Both dashed out of the box putting their helmets on as they left. Unfortunately one took size 6 7/8th, the other 7". The inevitable happened, one was temporarily blinded by too large a hat over his eyes while the other could hardly keep his on! There were few people about at the time so embarrassment was spared!

Helmets, being so tall could be cumbersome as well as protective. When driving station based cars for instance, helmets had to be worn, caps were for regular motor patrol officers only. One evening in the days of gas lighting in some houses in the town, a constable unwittingly scorched his tall helmet on a gas mantle while carrying out an enquiry. On another occasion a PC was caught in a deluge of rain and hail. He was wearing his helmet and cape at the time but because of the severity of the storm he put his cape, wigwam fashion, over his head and helmet and made his way to shelter being seen by one man who fled, terrified by the apparition coming towards him!

Police were called to investigate a complaint from the Vicar of Christ Church some years ago. Seemingly a local man, fond of his drink, would leave a local public house at closing time most nights of the week, usually the worse for wear. It became his habit to make a nuisance of himself in the doorway of the Church much to the annoyance of everyone. The beat PC kept watch and when he saw the man misbehaving he duly reported him for summons. It didn't work, for the man resumed his activities almost immediately. A plan was hatched, two policemen

Ornate uniforms with helmets – 1910-20.

hid themselves one night behind one of the gravestones placed around the Churchyard. Sure enough the offender returned to misbehave. The constables took off their helmets, placed their capes over their heads and with a high pitched 'Ooooooooohh' raised themselves up from behind the gravestone, The man ran, quickly, and was never seen again in the area. The Vicar, pleased with the outcome but not being aware of the circumstances thanked the beat PC, saying "I don't know what you said to that man, but it seems to have worked!"

During the long dark hours of nightshift, especially in wintertime, there were not many places for a patrolling policeman to take shelter or have a cup of tea. The gatehouses at Preston Hospital or Formica Factory served well but it was the all night bakeries which served best. Not just a cup of tea was available, but also the odd freshly baked bun or cake. In retrospect it is realised that the proprietors of bakeries welcomed the visit of the copper during the night to ensure the wellbeing of the staff. It was no chore, but a real pleasure. It was not without its hazards however, for on one occasion a PC entered the back door of a certain bakery just as a sack of flour was being lowered from an upstairs room to the bakery floor. The action of opening the door was sufficient to detract the sack from its intended course and empty the contents over the policeman! How do you explain that to the sergeant!

Another bakery, long since gone, worked nights, being noted for its fruit cakes. The stock of raisins was substantial and apparently two of the bakers were given to making raisin wine on the premises. The problem when making wine is to taste it and this, seemingly, is what the bakers did. Not being content with tasting, they imbibed enthusiastically, and when the night shift PC paid his visit there were no cakes being baked. Just two bakers totally inebriated. They were dismissed but when the beat officer pointed out to the management their dismissal would affect business, for they were good at their job, they were reinstated, giving assurances of their future abstinence.

It was not just the men who found themselves in situations which, although serious at the time could be laughed about later. The policewomen also were involved in humorous incidents. When Sylvia Rackham for instance took it upon herself to feed the flock of pigeons which tended to descend upon Norfolk Street, she could not have foreseen that as she threw crumbs out of an upstairs window for the birds, the Chief Constable would come out of his officer door just beneath. He couldn't help but smile as he dusted the crumbs from his tunic!

Dealing with sensitive issues was the domain of the policewomen. In a street close to the police station resided a lady who had a history of mental health problems. The Mental Health Officer was well versed with her case and visited frequently. One afternoon a call was received seeking police assistance at the lady's house. Knowing the lady well, two policewomen visited, but not wishing to cause undue distress they both put raincoats over their uniforms, and went to the house. Once inside the lady pointed to a broom standing in a corner and complained of it talking to her. With the aim of appeasing the lady, one PW bent down with her ear to the broom just as the Mental Health Officer entered. The MHO looked at the PW, mistaking her for the resident, and asked what she was doing. "Just listening to the broom", said the PW. "Never mind dear, I'll look after you," she said. The PW never listened to a broom again!

PC Joe Gunn was on duty in New York village late one night when he spotted a man riding a bicycle erratically. When stopped, the man was found to be drunk. He was duly arrested and he and the cycle were taken to the police station where a call had just been received from a concerned constable who had discovered his bicycle had been stolen from the rear of a police box. When charged with being drunk in charge of a pedal cycle and stealing the officer's cycle, the man said, "I can't remember". He remembered to turn up at court where he was fined and the cycle owner remembered to leave his bike in a safer place!

Later in his service Joe became Tynemouth's second dog handler with Herra, a German Shepherd. Living at the time on the Marden Estate, Joe had an arrangement with a local butcher to leave off-cuts of meat on a window sill for the dog, supplementing his diet. Some enterprising soul one day stole the meat from the sill while the family were out, probably thinking it was good, edible meat.

PC Joe Gunn with Police Dog 'Herra'.

No one (except the thief) knows whether or not he ate it, and if he did whether he realised what it was!

A former Chief Constable who retired in the 1940s was very fond of rearing hamsters. He would send his driver out into the countryside, armed with a scythe to cut the juiciest grass for his animals, and take it to his home to feed them. This of course was the same 'Chief' who managed the Isaac Black boot and shoe fund, a charity which ensured needy children of the Borough were properly clothed. The Chief was properly clothed, for photographs show him dressed in his Chief Constable's finery, complete with dress sword and cocked hat which he wore on special occasions, of which there appear to have been many. Most famous perhaps was the opening of the YMCA building in Churchway in 1937, by HM King George VI. Pictures show many dignitaries present for the event including the Chief Constable. As the official party made its way down some steps, the Chief's ceremonial sword caught one of the steps, unbalancing him. He quickly recovered and was unhurt, but one imagines some stifled sniggers from the on looking crowd.

Chief Constable Blackburn in attendance at the opening of the YMCA Building, Churchway by HM King George VI and Queen Elizabeth in 1937.

Policemen were given a 45 minute refreshment break during their eight hour shift in the 1950s. It was stipulated that the break must be taken in the beat box, at a specified time which differed from beat to beat. As some beats were more prone than others to people knocking on the box door if they saw a light on, a ploy was to switch the light off to enjoy a flask and a sandwich in peace. This was the case one night in Percy Main when a constable was having his 'bait'. Without warning there was a frightening crash outside the box and when the constable looked out he found a bus wedged under the railway bridge. The driver, who had stolen it from the nearby depot, was trapped inside. It was an easy arrest for the PC but his tea got cold.

One of the most dramatic incidents, quite funny at the time, but potentially dangerous was the 'Deer on the Pier'. One night a visiting rugby team to the area brought with them as a mascot a young deer. Things got out of hand and the animal was let loose, making its way to the Haven at Tynemouth. A call was received by the police from the pier watchman early the next morning informing them of the deer wandering towards the pier. PC John Jeffrey, who was on motor cycle patrol was first on the scene and sure enough saw that the deer was actually on the pier. John, with presence of mind, locked the iron gate on the pier minimising the risk of the animal running loose in Tynemouth. John was joined by PC John Norris and the two of them approached the deer which took fright (who wouldn't at the sight of two burly Tynemouth coppers) and galloped along the pier towards the lighthouse. Instead of stopping when it reached the pier end, the deer leapt over the wall straight into the sea and began swimming out. John Norris, a long serving member of Tynemouth Lifeboat Crew made his way rapidly to the lifeboat station where he launched the rubber inshore rescue craft. The two officers boarded the craft and chased after the deer which by this time was almost two miles out to sea and rapidly becoming exhausted. They managed to lift it into the boat and return to shore where the saturated deer was placed in a police van, taken to the station, dried off with towels and placed in a large kennel in the dogs home until the RSPCA collected it and returned it to the wild somewhere many miles from the sea!

Some serious moments, some humorous, but all part of the unexpected in the day of a Tynemouth officer.

CONSTABLES COURAGEOUS

Whether by chance, choice or persuasion, visitors to the former police station in Saville Street, North Shields, prior to its closure in 1976, could not help but notice in front of them, situated on a wall at eye level, an oak plaque measuring some 3' by 2', headed by the carved Borough Coat of Arms and containing, in gold leaf, the following inscription '1939-1945. IN HONOURED MEMORY OF THOSE FROM THIS FORCE WHO GAVE THEIR LIVES IN THE WORLD WAR' It then lists the following names:

PC 37 M.A. Clements.

Pilot Officer L. Cowell.

Trooper N.A. Daley.

F.R. 16 J.W. Hannah.

F.R 5 G.C. Murray.

Sgt Pilot W.T. Peverell.

The tribute ends with the words

'AT THE GOING DOWN OF THE SUN AND IN THE MORNING WE WILL REMEMBER THEM'.

The Memorial Plaque to Tynemouth officers who lost their lives in conflict. It hung, visibly for many years in the Saville Street Police Station.

There is nothing immediately unique in the memorial, after all, men and women from all walks of life died or were injured during the conflict and similar tributes were posted in many locations. This one however, in naming the Tynemouth policemen who gave their lives, identifies a broad background of expertise and experience. Of the six men named on the plaque two were RAF air crew, one a cavalryman, one a serving regular policeman who presumably was over age for active service and two First Reserve Constables, men who had completed their regular police service but who, because of hostilities, were unable to enjoy retirement being re-enlisted into full time police service where, because of enemy action, they lost their lives. One of them, F.R. Murray was in a police box in Charlotte Street one night when it suffered a direct hit, enemy airmen seemingly aiming for the nearby river and its prime targets.

These men, from diverse backgrounds and with equally diverse talents had a common bond, that of service to the community. The immediate post war years changed the structure of Tynemouth Police. Many still young men and one woman returned from war service and enlisted in the force. The wartime arrangements for policing were over and a new, well trained, disciplined and eager bunch of recruits took over from the wartime personnel.

During the following decade a similar intake of men and two more women were recruited to the force. In most cases the men had recently completed a period of National Service and were well prepared for the rigours of police duty and the potential dangers, the threat of which was ever present but fortunately seldom occurred. Patrolling in the dead of night checking business premises was a routine duty, but the slightest sound in an otherwise still night was often sufficient to trigger an adrenaline rush even though the sound was often made by cats going about their nocturnal business.

There were times, however, when odd noises in remote dark places were made by intruders, and the patrolling policeman, without personal radios at that time, had to make instant decisions to protect both the property he was examining and himself.

The usual outcome of these incidents was an arrest without violence, but there were exceptions. One that comes to mind happened at the foot of Howard Street, near Harbour View in the early hours of one morning. A patrolling constable checking D. Hill Carters' shop heard unusual sounds emitting from the premises. He investigated and was set upon by three men intent on breaking into the shop. In making good their escape they collectively assaulted the officer causing injuries, the result of which left scars both physically and mentally. The potential for this sort of confrontation was ever present and the single handed policeman needed an awareness of situations in which he found himself, and importantly, how to deal with them.

On commencing duty at a given time and location, a police officer had no way of knowing what the next eight hours had in store. Quite often the time was spent on mundane tasks which though not dangerous or hazardous, had to be carried out to ensure the safety and well being of the community living, working or visiting within the constable's beat boundaries. There were times however when the tranquillity of routine was broken. Such an incident took place one afternoon in 1958. PC 35 Ossie Burt was patrolling in Front Street, Tynemouth, when he was approached by a member of the public who informed him that some children were trapped in Collingwood Monument. Ossie ran to the scene through Bath Arcade and Priors' Park, and on reaching the monument he heard some shouts for help coming from the base of the structure.

He immediately asked a passer by to phone for the assistance of the Fire Service and he soon discovered that seeking adventure, two children had entered the labyrinth which forms the foundation of the monument by means of a disused door. They began exploring and one of them, a 14 year old boy, plunged 30 feet to the ground following the collapse of an internal wall, becoming trapped by the debris. The other boy was able to escape and raise the alarm. Obviously distressed, the trapped boy needed help fast. As it was not possible for Ossie to get through the disused doorway he climbed onto the plaza of the monument and found some loose paving stones. Gently lifting them up he was able to gain entry to the base. He took off his tunic, helmet and boots and with the aid of the Pier Watchman's portable searchlight he was able to edge his way along a crumbling ridge above the trapped boy.

A rope was found and Ossie was lowered down to the boy who by this time, although not seriously injured was extremely frightened. He calmed him and was able to fasten a rope around him, enabling the boy to be hauled to safety by other rescuers who had arrived at the scene. Once the boy was safe, Ossie then tied the rope around himself and he too was hauled to safety. The boy, scared but relatively unscathed,

The New Brick Built Section House, foot of Percy Park Tynemouth in the 1960s. PCs John Thompson, Ossie Burt and Danny Harrison are changing shifts.

was taken to hospital for treatment to an ankle injury and allowed home. It was later realised that because of falling crumbling masonry both he and his rescuer could well have been injured or worse.

The door was eventually bricked up to prevent further escapades and Ossie received the Testimonial on Vellum of The Royal Humane Society for his courage in risking personal injury in the rescue.

A former member of the Household Cavalry, Ossie Burt never lost his ability to handle horses. This was manifested early one morning in 1962 when two horses, one a large bay and the other a smaller grey, escaped from a field and caused havoc and mayhem along the roads adjacent to the Coast Road and the trading estate. Traffic was obliged to stop and in some cases take evasive action to avoid the animals, the larger of which decided upon a gallop along the Coast Road. The potential for injury to the public was great and sensing the danger, a motorist called the police. With a colleague, Ossie attended the scene, and in a police vehicle the officers were able to follow the larger horse until they came alongside. Ossie leapt from the police vehicle and successfully vaulted on to the back of the horse, riding bareback for a while until he brought the animal under control. He rode the horse to a nearby field, followed by the smaller grey, locked them both in and averted what may have become a serious incident. Little wonder that prior to his retirement, Ossie became Chief Inspector in charge of the Northumbria Police Mounted Branch!

Late one morning during the summer holidays of 1957, three youngsters, all aged about 11, decided upon an adventure at Cullercoats. The cliffs leading down to the beach proved ideal for the purpose and climbing soon began. It was an arduous task and tiredness soon replaced enthusiasm. The incoming tide was no respecter of tiredness or indeed small girls, and it was not long before the beat constable was called to the scene.

Things happened fast. A telephone call to Headquarters brought a patrol car driven by PC 19 Arthur Munden to the incident, and the services of a local garage proprietor were invoked resulting in the provision of a long length of towing rope. Within minutes Arthur had tied the rope around his waist, and while others held on at the cliff top, lowered himself to the trapped children bringing each one to safety. A Royal Humane Society Award made to Arthur was later presented by the Mayor of the Borough.

Arthur's disregard for his own safety was not surprising, after all he held the Military Medal for his bravery after escaping as a wartime 'desert rat' prisoner of war in 1943 and living behind enemy lines for over a year, causing, as he puts it, "mayhem to the enemy". On being demobilised he joined Tynemouth Police and soon became a motor patrol driver, being

PC Arthur Munden (right) receives his testimonial from the Mayor following his rescue of three girls in danger on the cliffs at Cullercoats. In the middle is Chief Inspector Tony Graham.

especially noted for his polite manner in dealing with offending motorists. He was regularly dubbed the 'courtesy cop' by the local newspaper!

The photograph on the next page is that of an ostensibly ordinary group of men, it is in fact a group of extraordinary men for it depicts the members of Tynemouth Police CID taken in the courtroom above the police station in the mid 1950s. Nothing particularly significant in a group photograph perhaps except that on the wall behind the group is a framed verse entitled 'The Prayer of a Horse'. It is uncertain why it hung there for many years or why it was put there in the first place but it is of interest as standing in the back row of the group and just to the right of the picture is Detective Constable Walter Wilkinson. Walter was awarded the Silver Medal and Citation Certificate of the Royal Society for the Prevention of Cruelty to Animals for the part he played in the early hours of one morning in 1966 when the Co-op stables in back West Percy street caught fire, trapping the horses. Walter, despite the dangers, broke the stable doors down and released the terrified animals. With one exception the horses escaped and proceeded to run amok through the town but were safely rounded up by a literal posse of policemen! None of the animals were physically hurt, maybe the Horse's Prayer was answered!

An interesting consequence appeared in the form of a letter of congratulation Walter received a little while later from an animal welfare group in the Philippines. The envelope bore the words 'Detective Wilkinson, England'. Despite the sparse detail, the letter was duly delivered!

Fires, especially in residences can be potentially dangerous and often, regrettably, fatal. Quite often the early hours of the morning are critical for that is when cigarettes or electrical appliances have been left burning and occupants become drowsy. It occasionally happened that a patrolling policemen in the dead of night would smell smoke or see flames and had to act both logically and rapidly.

Tynemouth CID Group, in the mid 1950s. The photographs was taken in Courtroom – The 'Prayer of a Horse' Plaque is behind them.

One such incident took place in Railway Street, North Shields during one night in 1958. A former hotel had been adapted to house the homeless on a casual basis and for a small sum, men could seek refuge overnight, sometimes with a bed other times in a chair, but always with a meal, shelter and warmth.

PC Cecil Broad was patrolling in the area when he was informed of a fire which had broken out in the hotel. He investigated and found the upstairs well alight. Residents were still inside the building and without regard for his own safety he called for assistance and entered the premises, escorting eight men from the increasing inferno. Others made their own escape while some were loathe to leave, it was the warmest they had been for some time!

Cecil was awarded a Certificate from the Royal Society for the Protection of Life from Fire, as were Sergeant Ron Burston, PCs Joe Gunn and Colin White, who performed equal acts of bravery in this and other incidents.

In exceptional circumstances police officers can be awarded what is regarded as the supreme accolade – The Sovereigns Commendation. The award is not given lightly, the actions of the recipient officer had to be exceptionally brave. To highlight the uniqueness of the award, only two Tynemouth Officers in the 119 year history of the force were bestowed. The outward sign of having been recognised by the King or Queen was the wearing of a silver oak leaf above the left breast pocket.

In the early 1950s, PWs 2 Mabel Ashley, always known as 'Mick' became the first Tynemouth officer to be given what was then the King's Commendation. A series of attacks on women in the Northumberland Dock Road area of the town caused great concern. The attacks were obviously the work of the same man, but despite observations by plain clothes men over a period of time, he evaded capture. As the incidents increased a new approach was planned. This involved the use of a policewoman. There were only two in Tynemouth at that stage, to act as a decoy. The strategy was successful as one dark night Mabel Ashley was walking down the Dock Road, closely observed by watching officers hidden in the undergrowth, when she was accosted by a man who attempted to assault her. A struggle ensued during which Mabel was injured. She revealed her identity but this only served to heighten the attackers resolve to escape and the struggle became more intense before the observing hidden officers were able to come to her aid. The man was arrested, charged and eventually convicted of a series of vicious attacks. In addition to being commended by the sentencing Judge, Mabel's actions were recognised in the receipt of the Royal accolade.

A similar award, this time the Queen's Commendation for Bravery was awarded in 1964 to PC 113 Robert Thompson. Bob was on motor cycle beat coverage on the outskirts of the town on the night of 29th December 1963 when a call was received at the police station of a domestic disturbance taking place in a house in the West Chirton area. Such calls were common enough and the usual procedure of directing the foot beat officer to the incident was followed. Normally by the time the officer arrived the disturbance had subsided and all was calm. This incident proved to be the exception for several other calls were made to the police asking for urgent help as an armed man was in a house holding the occupants hostage.

Although not on his beat, Bob answered the motorcycle radio and quickly attended the scene to be

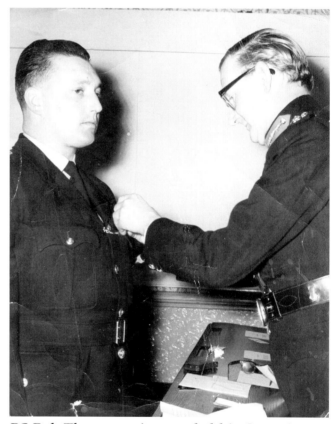

PC Bob Thompson is awarded his Queen's Commendation for bravery.

joined on arrival by PC 52 Alan Hudspith the dog handler, who had with him Tynemouth's first police dog, Lariat. Together they assessed the situation, discovering that the man was still in the house and was armed with a knife and a revolver. The man failed to respond to the officer's instruction to lay down his weapons and leave the house, and as the situation was becoming increasingly alarming in respect of the safety of the hostages, Alan broke a window and entered the house with Lariat. Bob, being aware of the dangers also entered the house and together with Alan overpowered and disarmed the man but not before Alan was stabbed in the arm. Following the prolonged struggle during which other officers sealed off the house, the man was arrested later receiving a custodial sentence.

In addition to Bob's award, Alan received the British Empire Medal with silver oak leaves for his bravery. This award to police officers is particularly rare and is indicative of the peril in which Alan placed himself that night. In October 1964 both officers received their respective awards from the Lord Lieutenant of Northumberland at a ceremony in the Town Hall in the presence of the then MP Dame Irene Ward, and Alderman Timothy Duff, the Chairman of the Watch Committee, and of course, Lariat!.

In earlier years of the history of the Tynemouth Force there were incidents of bravery performed by its members. Unfortunately time has erased many of the details, but there are two notable exceptions.

In 1913, Norman Ward joined the force as a constable but after less than two years he resigned to join His Majesty's Forces. He served in the Royal Army Medical Corp rapidly attaining the rank of acting sergeant. He applied for a commission and was enlisted into the Duke of Cornwall's Light Infantry as a second lieutenant in 1917. A few months later he was posted to France, where, in July 1918 he was leading his platoon over difficult ground attacking the enemy lines when he was hit by machine gun fire causing compound fractures of both the right tibia and fibula. Despite his wounds he continued to lead his men in their assault of the enemy lines.

His wounds resulted in amputation of the lower third of his right leg. He was repatriated back to England, where in 1919, after the cessation of war, he was medically discharged from the army.

Norman Ward returned to Tyneside where he was reinstated as a constable as was the requirement at that time. Usual practice for wounded men returning from the army to the police was a 'desk job' in civilian clothes. Not for Ward. He insisted on carrying out duties as a uniformed constable, eventually becoming a detective and retiring as a uniformed inspector. Despite his prosthetic lower limb, Inspector Ward earned both respect and admiration for the manner in which he carried out his duties. In later years he could be seen every morning, all year, swimming off Tynemouth Long sands, after taking off his wooden leg!

His military exploits earned him the award of the Military Cross, a high honour for gallantry, but then he was a Tynemouth Policeman whose collar number was also 52! In fact Alan Hudspith joined the force as Norman Ward retired and inherited his number.

Dame Irene Ward, then MP for Tynemouth, with the Lord Lieutenant of Northumberland and Alderman Timothy Duff, Chairman of the Watch Committee congratulate Alan Hudspith and Bob Thompson and of course Lariat.

On what one would expect to be a tranquil evening in late April, quite the reverse happened. The year was 1939 and as well as storms brewing over Europe, the sea off Sharpness Point at Tynemouth was equally boisterous. The Cullercoats lifeboat *Richard Silver Oliver* had been called out but fell foul of the raging waters and capsized. Six members of the crew perished. The number might have been more if two constables, PCs James William Carss and Frederick Millions, who had been alerted to the situation, attempted the impossible task of rescue. They swam out to the stricken lifeboat and were successful in assisting other crew members to safety, regardless of their own.

Inscribed silver watches were later presented to the two officers by the RNLI and, in addition, both were honoured to receive the Tynemouth Trust Silver Medal for their act of bravery.

These incidents highlight the dangers police officers found themselves in and the courage and inventiveness with which they dealt with them. The fact is that every time a police officer presented his or herself for duty they were potentially placing themselves in danger. No one knew what the next few hours had in store.

'END OF AN ERA'

Just as the chapter on 'Constables Courageous' was in the final stages of preparation, we were saddened to hear of the passing of Alan Hudspith who features extensively in the text. Alan, who was 84 years of age, was the only Tynemouth Policeman ever to receive the British Empire Medal for gallantry, and it is fitting to include this codicil a tribute to his memory.

After serving in the coal mines as a 'Bevan Boy' in the 1940s, Alan joined Tynemouth Police and served as a beat constable in all parts of the Borough. In 1956, following troubles on the island, Alan volunteered, and was accepted for service in the Cyprus Police, with the rank of sergeant. It was while serving in Cyprus that he became interested in the use of dogs for police purposes, being a keen observer of their use by the Military Police. He was especially fond of German Shepherds, seeing in them the potential for training in the civilian police.

Policewomen Judith Pyle and Sergeant Norman Walker stand in the doorway of Saville Street Police Station, 1966.

It was little wonder that a few years later when Tynemouth Watch Committee agreed to the request of the Chief Constable for a dog to be recruited, that the dog should be an Alsatian, and Alan should become Tynemouth's first police dog handler.

Lariat, or 'Larry' to his friends, was Alan's pride and very soon a bond developed between them both at work and at home. Larry became one of the family and was housed in a kennel at the rear of Alan's house. Larry could be aggressive to the wrongdoer at Alan's command and frequently was instrumental in the arrest of those offenders who chose not to obey the command to stop and decided to run. Not a wise move when Larry was about!

Sadly, the other Tynemouth officer involved in the armed hostage drama, Bob Thompson, died quite soon after Alan Hudspith.

Bob, a former member of the Household Cavalry who rode in the Queen's Coronation procession in 1953, and who finished his police service as an inspector in the mounted branch of the Northumbrian Force, will be remembered with affection by all who knew him as a devoted friend and fellow officer. It is equally pertinent to add this tribute to his memory, as he too was the epitome of a 'Constable Courageous'.

Tynemouth's first policewomen, Mary Bulman, receives a retirement gift from Chief Constable Walter Baharie in 1964 while her colleagues look on.

Born on the 1st of January 1850, the County Borough of Tynemouth Police served its public well. Starting with 12 under trained and under paid constables and finishing with 172 well trained, reasonably well remunerated but above all efficient personnel at midnight on Monday 31st March 1969. It served 119 years of community involvement which no doubt was upsetting to some residents or visitors at times, depending on their demeanour or 'mens rea' (state of guilty mind), but largely being welcomed, supported and valued by the majority it served.

The police station, part of the 1836 Town Hall building with the first floor courtroom, saw much activity during those years. The stone step at the entrance had worn to a concave as had the steps leading from the cells to the courtroom – the product of many years tramping of prisoners feet. The stout wooden door at the entrance had remained open for at least 140 years until the building finally closed in 1976 when the new Northumbria Police Station in Upper Pearson Street opened. When trying to finally close the door it fell of its rusted hinges. It is now bricked up, the building having been renovated for alternative use.

When I visited the old station a few years ago, just before the refurbishment, I found the substantial cell doors too were rust ridden and locked. Although, one could still see through the 'Judas hole' originally installed to check on prisoners well being. The inside of the cell was musty, the bench covered in dust and the toilet unmentionable. Strangely, the cell master key

"Sorry Madam, we're closed!" Sergeant John Jeffrey directs a customer to the new police station, January 1976.

which was always kept in a locked cabinet in the duty inspector's office, and now in my collection, was tried in the ancient door locking mechanism and opened it straight away.

The old charge room, once the hub of activity was unnervingly silent. The lamp room where Victorian policemen trimmed their lamps before night duty and which was later used as a makeshift kitchen, was dank, silent and eerie. What once was the best lit room in the station was now, paradoxically, the darkest. Memories from the past flooded through the mind – colleagues I had worked with, some notable prisoners, the old time coppers from days gone by, all momentarily appeared. The courtroom upstairs, now stripped of all its grandeur still reminded one of the cases heard over the years, sometimes acted out in an almost theatrical manner!

Progress had arrived attempting to erase the memories of the past, but to a former Tynemouth Borough Officer those memories are permanent. One is reminded of the motto of Tynemouth Borough, worn with pride on the helmet and cap badges 'Messis ab Altis, (Harvest from the Deeps)' (literal translation). I hope you have enjoyed this rich harvest of reminiscence from the depths of the memory of service with the County Borough of Tynemouth Police.

ACKNOWLEDGEMENTS

It is inevitable that in preparing a book of this nature one relies greatly on the information and assistance given by others. The content has been gleaned from my memory and that of many others, some of whom I had the pleasure of serving with and others who, until the early stages of preparation, were unknown to me. I have received a wealth of anecdotal recall, photographs and personal memories and experiences from many people for which I am indeed grateful. I particularly would like to thank the following for their input and enthusiastic encouragement:

Cecil Broad, Susan Burn, Ossie Burt, Roland Craig, Liz Crozier, Robert Davidson, Sandra Douglas, Mrs Gargett, John Grainger, Mrs A. Hewitt, Joan Hudspith, Michael Hudspith, John Jeffrey, Albert Kinnear, Arthur Munden, John Norris, David and Pat O'Flanagan, Violet Prudhoe, Judith Pyle, Sylvia Rackham, David Rattray, Robert Reay, Gordon Russell, Jack Short, John & Joy Smith, Gordon Southern, Charlie Steele, Ernest Storey, the late Robert Thompson, Clarissa Trevena, Norman Walker, May Wardhaugh, Mrs G. Whittle, Mr and Mrs Ward, Colin Wilkinson, Walter Wilkinson, Violet Wood, Harry Wynne, Andrew Young, North Shields Methodist Church.

Annual Police Flower and vegetable show in Howard Street Muster Rooms. Chief Constable and Mrs Scott congratulate members and their families.

My thanks to Pauline whose proof reading skills have yet again proved invaluable and to Janie for continued enthusiastic encouragement. If there are others whose names by error have been omitted, I hope you will accept my sincere apologies.

Finally, may I acknowledge the contribution of Kath Smith to this venture. Kath, who co-ordinates the 'Remembering the Past, Resourcing the Future' project at North Shields Library, instigated the work following the acquisition of a number of photographic images. She suggested the viability of building the collection to produce a book written around the images. Her continuing support and expertise, helped by Diane and Joyce of the Local Studies section of the Library, is valued and greatly appreciated.

Left: Tynemouth Flower Show in 1958. The van poised for action – conveying exhibits!